For Remi

Published by
Peter Bedrick Books
2112 Broadway
New York, NY 10023

Library of Congress Cataloging-in-Publication Data

Breebaart, Joeri
      When I die, will I get better? / Joeri and Piet Breebaart.
      Summary: A six-year-old boy tries to come to terms with the death of his younger brother by creating a story about rabbit brothers that closely parallels his own experiences.
      ISBN 0-87226-375-4
      1. Bereavement—Psychological aspects—Juvenile literature.
2. Brothers and sisters—Death—Psychological aspects—Juvenile literature.
3. Death—Psychological aspects—Juvenile literature. 4. Grief—Juvenile literature.
[1. Death—Psychological aspects. 2. Grief. 3. Brothers —Death—Psychological aspects.]
I. Breebaart, Piet.   II. Title.
BF575.G7B7344   1993
155. 9' 37' 083—dc20   93-2713

Printed and bound by Proost International Book Production, Belgium
10 9 8 7 6 5 4 3 2
First American edition

Preface

It seems so unfair that young children should have to encounter cruelty and illness, bereavement and loss. We would like them to be able to retain their innocence longer, to grow up with a sense of the world as a safe and reliable place, at least until that outlook was secure enough to withstand the inevitable impact of life's unfairness.

But life is not always that considerate. Children are born handicapped or come down with serious illnesses. Parents who desperately want to live, die and leave their children feeling abandoned. Siblings die, generating complex feelings of loss, guilt and vulnerability. What can we do in such cases, knowing that whatever we do will not be enough?

It seems to me that Joeri and Piet Breebart have it exactly right. At a time of great loss and sadness, children, like all of us, need consolation more than they need explanations. They need someone to hug them and hold their hand, not to confuse them with complicated medical explanations. They need validation, the reassurance that they have the right to cry and feel bad, that anyone in their situation would respond the same way. They need to be encouraged to talk, without revealing their soul in all its naked vulnerability. And more than anything else, they need to know that what you do with a tragedy is not explain it or justify it but survive it and draw from those around you the strength to want to go on living.

In a world where some children will die and some children will grieve, the Breebaarts give us what we need most.

Harold Kushner

When I Die, Will I Get Better?

Foreword

When Remi died of meningitis on December 25th 1991, he was two years and eight months old. Joeri was five and a half at the time. The two boys had shared a bedroom and they had been very close.

In the weeks after the funeral, Joeri was not only sad, but also very withdrawn and often angry. He was confused and disturbed by the loss of Remi and the concept of death and dying. He couldn't really talk about Remi's illness and death, and we had a hard time trying to reach Joeri and understand his feelings. We looked for children's books on death, but there wasn't much that appealed to us.

About six weeks after Remi's death, Joeri and I came to talk about Joe Rabbit. Joe was an invented character about whom we used to tell stories to Remi at bedtime. For Joeri, Joe stood for Remi. Joeri himself was Fred Rabbit, Joe's brother. Joeri said it was impossible to make up stories about Joe Rabbit now, since Remi was dead. I then suggested making up a story in which Joe would die. That was fine with Joeri.

Joeri created the story and always told me what he wanted me to draw for the next illustration. I then wrote down the story and made the drawing, sometimes the same day, sometimes a few days later. It was important to Joeri that I followed his indications. When, for example, I had made a fox for a doctor, he didn't agree, for the fox would eat the rabbits. No, the doctor ought to be an owl. There were also days, when Joeri didn't want to talk about it.

When I Die, Will I Get Better? describes Joeri's own experiences. How Remi got ill, how he died, the funeral, the loss, the coming to terms with the sadness. For us it meant a possibility to talk about it all with Joeri. It wasn't threatening this way. Joeri talked about the rabbits, and about us.

This healing process took about four weeks, and Joeri was very proud of the result. He told his teacher he had made a book about rabbits. Later he could tell her it was about his brother. He took the book to school and his teacher read it out loud in class. This meant a great deal to Joeri.

Piet Breebaart

When I Die, Will I Get Better?

Joeri and Piet Breebaart

Peter Bedrick Books
New York

Fred and Joe rabbit are brothers, who live at the edge of the wood. Joe is a happy little rabbit who likes playing with his friends. Neighbor Hedgehog enjoys keeping an eye on them. He can spend hours just watching them.

During the day Fred goes to school. Joe is still too young to go to school. When Fred comes home in the afternoon they play together until it's time for dinner.

One day Fred gets up, but Joe doesn't. He is ill. He has thrown up his food and his cheeks are burning hot with fever. Mother Rabbit says to Fred: 'Run quickly to Doctor Owl and ask him to come right away.'

Doctor Owl comes at once, examines Joe and says: 'He's got a high fever, but if you let him rest today, this little rabbit will feel a lot better tomorrow.'

Still, Mother Rabbit is very worried and stays inside with Joe.

When Fred comes home from school that afternoon, he finds all the animals gathered at his house. Even Father Rabbit is there.

Fred rushes inside. Joe is very, very ill. Everyone is upset. Never was there a young animal in the woods that was so ill.

Fred is sure that Doctor Owl will make Joe better. After all, Doctor Owl knows everything.

Fred stays inside. He watches Joe in his bed. He doesn't want to be outside with all the other animals.

That night, while Doctor Owl and Father and Mother Rabbit are standing at Joe's bed, Joe dies. Mother Rabbit holds Joe. Everyone is crying. Fred is standing in a corner, he doesn't understand any of this. Why are they crying? He thinks it all frightening, but he doesn't cry.

Owl says: 'Joe was too ill, I couldn't save him.'

Later all the animals come in. They stand around Joe and watch his little white face. They can't believe he's dead and they all cry.

Then Piglet comes and says: 'Now you don't have a brother anymore, Fred, how awful!'

But Fred thinks: Doctor Owl will surely make Joe better in the morning. He wants to go outside and play in the woods with Piglet.

The next day Father Rabbit takes the Mole family to the little field in the middle of the woods. Father Rabbit wants Joe to be buried there. They choose a beautiful spot, next to a patch of red flowers. The Moles spend the whole day digging, but they don't mind; they are happy they can help the Rabbits.

Before Joe can be buried, a coffin needs to be made, and who is a better carpenter than Beaver? Beaver does his very best to make a good coffin.

Fred is not in the mood for playing. He has joined Neighbor Hedgehog on his bench. Fred says: 'When I die, will I get better?'

'No,' says Neighbor Hedgehog. 'Animals only die once, but mainly when they're as old as I am. It wasn't really Joe's turn yet.' Fred begins to understand it just a little. 'So, I can never play with him again,' he says.

'No, only in your mind, when you think of him,' says Hedgehog.

Fred feels tears coming to his eyes. 'And what will happen with Joe now?'

'We will bury him in the little field in the woods. Everyone will be there and a few animals will say something about Joe,' says Hedgehog.

'Then I want to say something too,' says Fred.

'That's a very good idea,' says Neighbor Hedgehog.

The night before the funeral Fred has a dream. He dreams of Joe's coffin gliding through a tunnel to the grave. Joe and Fred and all their friends glide with it. It goes very fast, and is fun!

When Fred wakes up, the tunnel has gone and he feels lonely and sad.

Fred gets up early. His mother and father are already up and about. Fred gets Joe's favorite toys and some of his books. Then he writes on a slip of paper what he wants to say about Joe. He knows exactly what he wants to say, but it is difficult to find the right words.

They stay in the room with Joe until the other animals come to take him to his grave.

Together they walk to the field in the middle of the woods. The coffin is lowered into the hole. Most animals don't want to leave Joe yet and they climb into the hole with the coffin. When father and mother say how sweet Joe was and how they miss him, all the animals cry.

Then it's time for Fred to read his letter. He can hardly speak because of the lump in his throat. Fortunately his father holds him. Fred says: 'Joe, I've put your best car and your favorite books in the coffin with you, so you won't have to get bored when you are alone. We'll come and play in this field every day, close to you. Maybe you'll hear us. Bye, sweet Joe.'

The first few days after the funeral Father and Mother Rabbit stay home. They can only think about Joe; they're too sad to do anything at all.

Fred doesn't want to play. He walks through the woods all by himself. He can't help thinking of Joe all the time and that makes him cry. But he doesn't want to cry. It makes him angry. He's angry with everyone.

The animals want to help the Rabbits. Father Pig is a good cook. He says: 'Come and have dinner with us any time.' The Rabbits go, but they are not very hungry. Still, they like to be with their friends. It helps.

Everyday father and mother feel a little better, and so does Fred. He wants to play with Piglet again and he isn't so angry anymore.

On the first sunny day, Fred and his friends go and play on the little field where Joe has been buried. They are having fun again for the first time since Joe died. Beaver has made them a swing. Neighbor Hedgehog thinks the field a good place for his bench. When he watches the friends play he is happy. He hears Fred and his friends laugh again. A sound he hadn't heard for a long, long time.